465202977

This play was first presented by the New York Shakespeare Festival, Joseph Papp, Director, on February 8th, 1975 with the following cast:

CAST

ROB	*Guy Boyd*
BILL	*Tom Lee Jones*
SHELLY	*Lindsay Crouse*
MARY-ELLEN	*Kathryn Grody*
DANE	*John Heard*
RORY	*Ray Barry*
REILLY	*Ed Seamon*

The actions of the play happen in one day somewhere on the coast of the Pacific Northwest. 1974.

The play was directed by *Peter Gill*
Set was designed by *Pat Woodbridge*

Fishing

ACT ONE

SCENE 1

A living room in a rented shack on the Pacific Coast. Bare feeling, a transient place being made permanent. Couch, a few tattered easy chairs, eating table, bookcase with mildewed books and a few new ones, mostly paperbacks. Franklin stove. Indian rug. Against wall a .22 rifle, a cavalry sword, three fishing rods. Portable Sony TV. And like that. It's morning. It's drizzling. The Northwest. ROBBIE sleeps on the couch with a powder-blue sleeping bag pulled over him and an open book on the floor.

Lights up. Enter BILL holding an egg. He sees ROBBIE asleep. Checks him out. Makes a loud rooster noise. ROBBIE stirs. BILL walks around the room, strutting and crowing like a rooster. He stops.

ROBBIE. Oh shit. Is it Tuesday?

BILL. Wednesday, m'boy. No, wait. It's July, definitely.

ROBBIE. Let's skip today. I want to have tomorrow, O.K.

BILL. O.K., it's tomorrow. Look what I got.

ROBBIE. (*Looking.*) Small . . . whitish object. Spheroid. I give up.

BILL. An egg. I found it underneath the chicken out in the coop.

ROBBIE. Coincidence. Eggs come from Safeways. I hate waking up.

5

BILL. Our chicken has laid a egg. A white egg. And just wait'll you taste it. Country chicken eggs are amazing, young Rob. They are tasty and they are funky and they are real.

ROBBIE. You know what I think.

BILL. You just don't want to admit country living is far out. Well, you're wrong cause country living happens to be far out and if you don't believe me read your Whole Earth Catalogue and your crazy Ewel Gibbons and you'll see it written in plain undeniable black and white.

ROBBIE. Shelly put that egg under the chicken.

BILL. Now why would a nice girl like Shelly go and do a deceitful thing like that?

ROBBIE. Cause you said you'd chop off its head and serve it for dinner if it didn't crank an egg out by today.

BILL. How come you're sleeping in here?

ROBBIE. My room's haunted. I was having a nightmare.

BILL. Want to shoot some gophers?

ROBBIE. No.

BILL. Want to go fishing? High tide's 10:27. I got bait.

ROBBIE. I was in a boat. I was fishing off the back. Some guy was in the cabin steering. I thought it was you but it wasn't. I knew him. There were these shoes underwater. Filled with snot. I couldn't focus on them. Then we were on Eighth Avenue, and we were still in the boat and I was fishing for wads of newspaper. I wanted to stop and look at the newspaper cause there were stories about me in these newspapers but the guy in the cabin wouldn't stop, wouldn't slow down. I want to sleep.

BILL. Me too.

ROBBIE. What?

BILL. I had the same dream.

ROBBIE. Leave me alone.

BILL. Remember when you used to dream about flying and cowboys and chicks with wet sissies.

ROBBIE. Yeah. Sheeet. (*Spits.*)

BILL. Sheeet. (*Spits.*) Shelly dreamed she had a job. She's really upset. It was sort of a nightmare.

ROBBIE. Well, we've had dreams now. Time for emptying of the bowels and cleansing of the skin. Another day, another trip. Where's Shelly? (ROBBIE *begins dressing.*)

BILL. Safeways. Morning milk run. And by the way, in case you forgot, last night Reilly said he was gonna come today.

ROBBIE. Oh, shit, Reilly. That's real life, isn't it.

BILL. Yep. Time for a joint.

ROBBIE. That's going to be a problem because I smoked the last of our stash last night. I couldn't sleep.

BILL. Things are really getting desperate. Like twenty-one fifty-seven in the bank desperate. And no dope.

ROBBIE. And not a whole lot of food either.

BILL. Fuck food, I'm talking basics.

ROBBIE. At least we got eggs. One a week at the present rate. That is, if Shelly isn't behind this sudden mysterious egg phenomenon.

BILL. I figure we can get Reilly down from fifteen hundred. I don't think the boat's worth that. If we go really heavy on the condition the boat's in I bet we can jew him down to a thousand.

ROBBIE. Twenty-one fifty-seven in the bank. You're the jew, you do the talking.

BILL. Maybe nine hundred.

ROBBIE. That's nine with two zeros after it.

BILL. We're a nice bunch of kids.

ROBBIE. Straight from the shoulder, I have reservations.

BILL. We can dig up a thousand. There's gotta be a way. I mean between you and me and Shelly, and maybe someone else'd come in for a share like maybe crazy Rory the undertaker.

ROBBIE. I'm talking more about Reilly's boat. I mean, I'm not exactly an old salt or anything, but if we're gonna do commercial salmon fishing we have to have a boat with certain basic things, right, like a tendency to stay on top of the water. I heard Reilly's boat sunk three times last winter.

BILL. Yeah, but that was at the dock, that wasn't out on the ocean.

ROBBIE. Is that supposed to make me feel better?

BILL. Boats leak. You gotta be around them so you can bail them out. If you're not there, of course they'll sink.

ROBBIE. I'd really like a boat that didn't sink. Even when you weren't there.

BILL. All boats leak.

ROBBIE. How do you know so much about boats all of a sudden. Listen, pal o' mine, it just so happens I've read all kinds of sea-faring books, and the one distinguishing factor about all the major historical ocean-going hot shits is they all had boats that floated, dock or no.

BILL. You always sit around figuring out the bad news, don't you. Ever since you got here.

ROBBIE. I just know your dreams, Billy-boy. I can see your fleet of five hundred fully automated vacuum cleaner-type fishing tankers with radar-equipped salmon detectors and canning plants in the hold and stereophonic P.A. blasting out Pink Floyd on the quarter deck or whatever the fuck you call it, William-Acid-Rock-Where-Did-The-Sixties-Go-Barenberg Pacific Salmon Outta Sight Enterprises, Inc.

BILL. Some of us don't have lots of bread in the family, fuckhead. Some of us have to make a living.

ROBBIE. My old man's bread is not *my* bread. Leave me alone.

BILL. Come on, bummer, don't tell me you haven't

heard that old ocean calling. You're the one that sat out there on Angel's Point all day, and all night, and all the next day staring at it when you first got here. Ah, Silence. High tide, calm sea, beer and dope and some funky sounds on the cassette, sea trout crawling up your line begging to be fried in bread crumbs with a little garlic and sage. I'm telling you, man, that old ocean is just one great big mama with a smile on her face and food in her belly. All we need is a boat and a few smarts and she'll lay great abundance upon us at seventy-nine cents a pound and that adds up.

ROBBIE. Ho-hum, another day, another trip.

(SHELLY *enters with brown bag.*)

SHELLY. Guinevere is a loser.

ROBBIE. Guinevere.

BILL. Shelly named the chicken.

ROBBIE. Guinevere?

SHELLY. Why not. It's a good chickeny name. Now all she's gotta do is lay an egg once in a while and we'll be in business. I really thought today'd be the day. So, what's happening?

BILL. Shelly-pie(?)

SHELLY. What?

BILL. Shelly-pie(?) . . .

SHELLY. What's on your mind?

BILL. There's something mighty suspicious about your sudden interest in Guinevere's egg-laying career.

SHELLY. I just wondered if she laid one.

ROBBIE. Watch out, it's a trap.

BILL. Did you put an egg underneath Guinevere's body this morning?

SHELLY. She laid an egg?!! Guinevere laid an egg?! Oh, Guinevere you little sweetie-pie. I knew she'd figure it out. Didn't I say she'd come through in the end. Where is it. Let's see.

ROBBIE. Stand back with awe.

(BILL *raises the egg slowly. He and* ROBBIE *do the "Also Sprach Zarathustra" theme from "2001."*)

SHELLY. Guinevere is a genius. She definitely gets an extra cup of scratch today and I'm going to knit her some booties.

BILL. Shelly-pie?

SHELLY. I mean two years of art school and I could never do an egg like that. It'll have to be scramble for three ways . . . I'll make some bread for toast.

BILL. You're avoiding me, Shelly-pie.

SHELLY. Why am I avoiding you?

BILL. Did you slip this egg under Guinevere so I wouldn't chop off her head today? Did you?

SHELLY. I bet she lays an egg tomorrow. Another one.

BILL. That's not what I asked.

SHELLY. How come you always think I'm doing something sneaky?

BILL. Shelly-pie honey sweet baby cake. (BILL *advances on* SHELLY. *An old game.*)

SHELLY. Oh dear! Help! No, no, please don't. Oh! Oh! Oh! (BILL *tickles her. She shrieks, but you know.*) Leave my body alone. I have a surprise.

BILL. You were a very naughty Shelly-pie, weren't you.

SHELLY. No. Yes. Yes.

BILL. Yes, what?

SHELLY. Yes I was.

BILL. Yes I was what?

SHELLY. Yes I was a very naughty Shelly-pie, wasn't I. Now stop it and I'll tell you what I got.

BILL. Repeat ten times I was a very naughty Shelly-pie.

SHELLY. I was a very naughty Shelly-pie. I was a very naughty Shelly-pie. I was a very naughty Shelly-pie. I was a very naughty Shelly-pie. I was a very naughty Shelly-pie. I was a very naughty Shelly-pie.

I was a very naughty Shelly-pie. I was a very naughty Shelly-pie. I was a very naughty Shelly-pie.

BILL. That was only nine.

SHELLY. I have my pride. Yikes, stop.

ROBBIE. Who wants a third of a scrambled egg. (BILL *and* SHELLY *stop.*)

SHELLY. Oh. Hi, Rob.

BILL. Rob isn't feeling all kinds of positive today. He wants it to be a bummer, so we have to do everything in our power to help him out.

SHELLY. (*To* ROBBIE.) For real?

ROBBIE. I don't know. The weather's sort of shitty and Reilly's coming and we don't have a thousand dollars for a boat that keeps sinking anyway and on top of that this house is haunted by evil spirits.

SHELLY. Are these the reasons you're not feeling positive?

ROBBIE. I'm horny.

BILL. Ah, that's the reason you're not feeling positive.

ROBBIE. We're out of smokeables.

BILL. Anything else?

ROBBIE. And we're a lost generation in search of meaning but unable to grasp a sense of values in a shipwrecked century.

SHELLY. That's true, but then again, fuck it. Let's have an egg.

ROBBIE. Can I use your room.

SHELLY. Sure.

ROBBIE. If the weather clears up, and a girl comes by who wants to get laid and we get our hands on some dope and Reilly decides to sell for twenty-one fifty-seven, then wake me up. (ROBBIE *exits.*)

BILL. Bummerville, oh, bummerville. (*Hummed, that is.*)

SHELLY. I can never tell when he's being serious.

BILL. The thing about Rob is he's full of shit. You know that, you know Rob.

SHELLY. Why? I mean you're probably right . . . or wrong, but why? You're the man, hon, so what you say goes, but like why is he full of shit as opposed to you or me.

BILL. He wouldn't give a damn if this whole fishing thing fell through.

SHELLY. I bet he would.

BILL. I bet he wouldn't.

SHELLY. I bet he would.

BILL. I bet he wouldn't.

SHELLY. I bet . . . (BILL *dives for her, more tickles.*) Hey don't. (*Pause.*) You asked him to come out here. I mean, he is your best friend and everything.

BILL. He doesn't have to do anything. He just goes around having a groovy time and spending his old man's money. If he had to like work, you know. If he needed the bread . . . I could maybe feel more like trust. That's all I mean. He's a good guy. I dig him.

SHELLY. What if it doesn't work out with the boat?

BILL. It'll work out.

SHELLY. I know, baby, but what if it doesn't.

BILL. Like crazy Rory says, "Wow, man, you want to get into something you like, put your energy right there and the whole thing just happens, right." (*Pause.*) It just has to work. It feels right. What can I say? Just being out there on the ocean with no one to hassle you. No assholes trying to get rich and coming down on you cause you don't want their fucking crazy trip. Just me and Rob and the fish. Us and them. And the boat.

SHELLY. As the sun sinks slowly in the West.

BILL. So it's romantic. Nothing wrong with that. Nothing at all. I'll wear a cowboy hat, so what.

SHELLY. The farm was sort of romantic.

BILL. That was different.

SHELLY. Why?

BILL. It just was. A farm is just a bunch of dirt and cows shitting in the fields. I'm not a land person. I'm a water person. Pisces. Why the fuck is everyone closing in on me today, I'm a nice guy.

SHELLY. Hey, I wasn't closing in, baby. I think it's a fine idea. And I think it's going to work out really good. The old Ching said "After Initial Setbacks, Great Abundance."

BILL. You throw it?

SHELLY. Yeah, last night.

BILL. Well all right, all right. That's better. In fact, that's kind of far out. That definitely calls for an egg, and a little smokeroo. Oh, shit.

SHELLY. Just sometimes I don't know I think about it. About how things don't work out sometimes or not not work out exactly more like not work out exactly the way you want them to. Or even work out but not be what you thought they'd be. And how you adjust. I know you have to fight. I know that. But you oughta be able to get your head into a place where whatever's happening around you . . . outside of you . . . it's O.K. It's just O.K. no matter which way things go. Anyway, I know what I mean. It's like, some people always go around looking for a beautiful place to be in and other people make whatever place they're in beautiful. (BILL *laughs*.) It's not funny.

BILL. In case you forgot, Shelly-pie, I read that book, too, and it's not like I don't dig Swami whatever his name is. A lot of my favorite gurus are fat little Indians but all that stuff is bullshit.

SHELLY. It is not.

BILL. It is too.

SHELLY. You don't know what you're talking about.

BILL. (*Pause.*) I hope we get some sun today. (*Pause. Truce.*)

SHELLY. I got peyote.

BILL. Did you say something?

SHELLY. Yup.

BILL. As in the psychedelic-parts-of-certain-cac-tusses-native-to-the-American-Southwest peyote?

SHELLY. Cactii. Yup.

BILL. What how when where why?

SHELLY. That chick that's always at the marina, the hippie chick with that weird lizard. She was in Safeways over by frozen foods. I was just getting milk and she came up and said, "Hey, man, I've seen you around, you want some dynamite peyote, man, hey, man," you know, and she handed me a bag, a hundred buttons. They picked 'em last week in Arizona "or Chicago, or something, like they grow, right." Boy, was she out of it. And the manager guy that always tails you when you're shopping—

BILL. Shit-Shoes.

SHELLY. Yeah, Shit-Shoes, he's standing right at the end of the aisle and he knew what was going down and he was shitting in his shoes because if he hassled her there'd be a big hippie-drug scandal in Safeways and you can't have a big hippie-drug scandal in Safeways. So I gave her ten bucks. That's fair.

BILL. A hundred buttons for ten bucks. Jesus. That's disbelievable. Let me see.

(SHELLY *takes them out of the bag and shows them.*)

SHELLY. Did I do good, huh-huh?

BILL. They're fresh! They're not even dried. They're juicy and green and sunkist and Shelly, you're a genius. I knew there was a reason I kept you around.

SHELLY. Aw gee.

BILL. God in his infinite wisdom and mercy has seen fit this day to lay upon us the means to get very stoned for many hours, and if I can jew Reilly down to a thousand today, I say we celebrate with a trip of unforgettable magnitude and duration.

SHELLY. Sounds like a good plan.

BILL. *Far out!* O.K. Time for the cooking and the eating of the breakfast. What's for food.

SHELLY. Ah. That's the hitch. See, after I gave the lizard chick the money I realized an embarrassing thing.

BILL. You silly girl.

SHELLY. I got milk. We can have coffee. And an egg. And milk.

(RORY *enters. He's 30-ish. Red and black lumber-man's shirt and jeans. Soaking wet from the rain. Bottle of beer in hand. He's drunk.*)

RORY. First thing is I gotta pee and how are you and where's the party.

SHELLY. Hi, Rory, how's tricks.

RORY. Tricks is tricks and kicks is kicks and always the twain shall meet as the chipmunk said to the tractor. What? Whew. All *right.* Yeah. Water. There seems to be a little water around here and most of it's on me. Must be raining, know what I mean. The big boy is taking a pee. On you and me. And that makes three. Yessiree. How bout some tea. Whew, nine o'clock a.m. in the morning and I'm already drunk as a skunk in a bunk.

BILL. Sit down, Rory. Or kneel or something so you don't have far to fall.

RORY. Right, right. (*Sits.*) So how's your ass and pass the grass.

BILL. We're all out.

RORY. Whew, tragedy-tragedy-tragedy. Famine in the lamine.

BILL. Don't you have any?

RORY. (*German.*) Do I heff der grass geschmoken? Nein mein hippeez. It's juice all the way 'till the end of the day, and I definitely have to do something about the urino in my bladdero.

SHELLY. Why don't you go to the toilet.

RORY. I like that girl, yes I do. You oughta be in the toilet business. I'll have some grass for you a little later. Hey, I want you to remember something. Six-thirty. Remember that. Six-thirty. Very important time of the day. Big changes at six-thirty.

SHELLY. O.K. What about six-thirty, Rory.

RORY. You want to know and here we go. Party-arty-o at the big house on the cemetery.

SHELLY. Again?

RORY. Dass raht, missy-Shelly. Gotta play de fiddle while de ciddy burns. Lotta foods gonna happen. Big salad, apple crumble, and Delores is doing this whole number with a twenty-five pound Ling Cod all wrapped up in pastry and baked for two hours.

BILL. Twenty-five pound Ling Cod? Where the hell did you catch that?

RORY. We haven't caught it yet. That happens this afternoon. And I got these friends coming by from the movie said they'd be bringing some dynamite mari-hootee from the land of Mehico. Mucho bene. (*Pause.*)

BILL. You got any spare bread, Rory.

RORY. For Reilly's boat? No way.

BILL. How'd you know about that?

RORY. Reilly ain't so wiley. Word's out you guys want to go fishing. How the fuck you think you're gonna keep anything from the undertaker in a town this size. Leave the fish alone. That's what the fish are saying. "No, no, no, you groovy dudes, don't catch me don't sell me." What do you want to fish for? I mean—I mean—I mean, go fishing. That's all. Just go down to Angel Point and catch a few, eat a few. It's fun. But, man, go commercial? Leave the ocean alone. It's having a good time.

BILL. Thanks for the help.

RORY. Come on, amigo, I bum you not out. O.K.,

here's the deal. Why is Reilly selling? That's uno. Why's he selling so cheap? That's dos. And why's he in such a hurry? That's trey and you're out.

BILL. You know about something we don't know about?

RORY. Reilly's a corpse. He can still do the boogaloo, but he's dancing his last dance. Where does I work? I works in the graveyard. What do I do? I plants folks. Reilly's wife has a little deal going and I'll tell you about it but you never heard it, you dig?

BILL. Are you sure about Reilly?

RORY. His brain got all full of little cloteroos and one day they're just not gonna stay put and then (pop!), bye-bye Reilly. And since my graves is all the rave Missus Reilly comes to me and pays me to dig a grave pre-advanso of the big day. It's all dug. Last week. Whew. Got a piece of canvas over it keep the rain out. All he gotta do is crawl in and I dump the turf on him. And see, I don't have a whole lotta mind to invest in a boat when I just dug a hole for the man that owned it. I ain't superstitious, you understand, but I am superstitious.

BILL. Fuck.

RORY. Heaviness.

SHELLY. Well, yeah, sort of, but it's not our fault that he's dying. We can't do anything about that and we could probably get him to come down a couple hundred since he has to sell.

RORY. You just care too much, baby, that's your hang-up.

SHELLY. Someone's gonna get the boat. And anyway, he's just dying, it's not all that big a deal. People die all the time. Forget it. Bill.

RORY. Six-thirty. Party at the graveyard. I gotta pee, yessiree.

(MARY-ELLEN and DANE stand awkwardly in the kitchen doorway.)

MARY-ELLEN. Excuse me, is Rob here?

RORY. Hey, you guys were driving around in a red Volvo.

DANE. That's right.

RORY. I saw you on the way over and I thought wow, they're lost, whew! How the hell are you?

DANE. Fine. The door was open so we just let ourselves in.

RORY. What's the word on Volvos? I been thinking of getting one.

DANE. We're pretty happy with it.

RORY. That's good to know. What time is it.

SHELLY. It's nine-thirty.

RORY. Nine-thirty and I is smashed out of my grapefruit. Gotta get this day together. Pee first, pay later. Arriverderci. Chiao. Gutten Tag and kung fu. Scusi. (*He brushes past* MARY-ELLEN *and* DANE. *Stops. All cramped in doorway.*) About twenty-five a gallon.

DANE. What? Oh, yeah, we've been doing about that. A little more on long trips.

RORY. Beautiful beautiful. (*He exits.*)

MARY-ELLEN. I hope we didn't interrupt anything. I mean I hope this is the right place.

SHELLY. You're friends of Rob.

MARY-ELLEN. He stayed with us before he came here. We just decided to drive up. You didn't have a phone or anything.

BILL. He's asleep.

MARY-ELLEN. Oh.

DANE. We could come back later.

MARY-ELLEN. Maybe we could wake him up. Could you tell him that Melon and Dane are here to see him.

BILL. Do you guys have any dope?

SHELLY. I'll wake him up.

BILL. I don't think you should. The sun's not out yet.

MARY-ELLEN. Is he all right?

SHELLY. What do you mean?

MARY-ELLEN. Rob.

SHELLY. You mean like is he sick or something?

DANE. I guess we ought to come back later.

SHELLY. Did you say Melon?

MARY-ELLEN. It's Mary-Ellen, but no one's called Mary-Ellen, right, so it's Melon. Cute, huh.

BILL. The thing about Rob is he's sort of hiding for the day cause he's horny and depressed and we're out of smokes and he's pretty sure the house is haunted.

MARY-ELLEN. Same old Rob.

DANE. Maybe I ought to bring the car around. (*Enter* ROBBIE.)

ROBBIE. (*Casual.*) Hi. Listen, Rory's peeing on the side of the house—and it stopped raining. (*Pause.*) Have a nice trip up?

MARY-ELLEN. Yes, thank you, shithead.

(MARY-ELLEN *and* ROBBIE *bust up laughing and screaming.* DANE *smiles. They all hug each other.* SHELLY *and* BILL *look at each other. Fade.*)

(*End of* SCENE 1.)

ACT ONE

SCENE 2

Front of the house, porch and yard. Lots of farm-type junk on the porch. Maybe a makeshift birdhouse on a post.

Bright sunlight. MARY-ELLEN *is sunning herself, eyes closed, face up.* SHELLY *is shooting at an Offstage target with the .22.*

SHELLY. (*Fires.*) Bulls-eye. Guess we're about ready for the bank job. Hey, Bill, I hit three out of ten.

BILL. (*Inside.*) Don't waste bullets.

SHELLY. Mah man.

MARY-ELLEN. (*Continue.*) I guess it's just my imagination. Eight years, though, that's a long time. And the way he's been going around visiting all his old friends. I mean it's great that he feels like doing that but sometimes . . . like when he stayed with us, you couldn't tell if it was more of a hello-visit or a goodbye visit.

SHELLY. Well, if I was gonna pick someone to worry about . . . and I never would unless I really had to . . . it wouldn't be Robbie.

MARY-ELLEN. We're not really worried.

SHELLY. Want to try a few shots?

MARY-ELLEN. No thanks, I don't like guns.

SHELLY. I didn't used to, but now I love 'em. Not really, but I feel it becomes a young woman of today to be handy with a rifle. I cook and sew too. I'm sort of Renaissance-y. (*Fires.*) Shit.

MARY-ELLEN. Do you feel anything?

SHELLY. I haven't exactly seen God or anything but I had a few rushes.

MARY-ELLEN. I feel like I'd sort of like to puke, but I don't really want to do that. If I'd already puked I'd probably feel better than I do.

SHELLY. How many buttons did you take?

MARY-ELLEN. Five. I've never done peyote before. I'm not sure what's supposed to happen.

SHELLY. I had eight. I feel pretty good.

MARY-ELLEN. I feel pretty nauseous.

SHELLY. Let's not talk about it.

MARY-ELLEN. I'm sorry.

SHELLY. Hey, I don't mean to be like heavy about it. I mean. Shit. (*Controlled.*) I don't like to know when people are feeling sick because that's something they have to deal with and there's nothing you can do about it. (*Pause.*) Wow. That was great. That was exactly what I wanted to say. That doesn't happen a lot. (GUENIVIERE *clucks Offstage.*)

MARY-ELLEN. What's that?

SHELLY. (*Going around house.*) I'm coming, baby, I'm coming.

ROBBIE. (*He enters.*) Any reports from the land beyond the shadows?

MARY-ELLEN. I don't know about this peyote. How do you feel?

ROBBIE. Fan-fuckin'—tastic. Look at that sun. It's weird the way the weather keeps changing around here. God, that mountain. I'm sure it wasn't that close to us yesterday.

MARY-ELLEN. Rob.

(*Enter* SHELLY. *with* GUENIVIERE *in her arms.*)

ROBBIE. Any more eggs yet?

SHELLY. She's doing O.K. Don't hassle her. She's no good under pressure. (*To* MARY-ELLEN.) Have you met Gueniviere? You can hold her if you want to.

MARY-ELLEN. (*Backing off.*) Please take her away. I'm sorry. I just have a thing about chickens. (SHELLY *goes off.* BILL *enters.*)

BILL. How ya feeling?

ROBBIE. Like shit in a swamp. I'll tell you something. Peyote may turn out not to be my gateway to the beyond.

BILL. I feel like another shit in a swamp.

ROBBIE. Hi there. What's a nice shit like you doing in a swamp like this?

MARY-ELLEN. Where's Dane?

ROBBIE. Dane? Dane? Where'd you go, Dane. Dane, baby, come to papa. (ROBBIE *looks in his shirt pocket, his pants pocket, takes off his shoe, looks there.* BILL *and* SHELLY *join in. This is hysterical.*)

BILL. Come on out, Dane, we know you're around here somewhere.

ROBBIE. Hey, Shelly, what'd ya do with Dane.

SHELLY. I didn't mean to eat him. I'm sorry, I'm sorry. There was only one egg.

ROBBIE. Ah, come to the scenic Northwest and groove.

MARY-ELLEN. Has anyone seen Dane? Sometimes he wanders.

SHELLY. Dane's here.

(DANE *stands in the front door holding a cutting board with buttons on it, like a serving tray.*)

DANE. O.K. I think I've figured it out. We're feeling sick because of the strychnine in these buttons. Strychnine is a convulsant and it's chemical action is to make the stomach tense up. Now the other thing that happens is the actual hallucinogenic effect of the drug that's in this stuff, and I'm not sure what that is, but there's a point where the curve traced by the poison and the curve traced by the high cross each other and from that point on the high is predominant. And this depends on the dose. Now there's less strychnine than there is drug so it stands to reason that the more you take, the less chance there is of getting sick.

ROBBIE. Good thinking.

DANE. Yes. So what I've done is I've brought out more buttons.

SHELLY. Those are our buttons.

BILL. Cool it, Shelly.

SHELLY. But that's our peyote.

DANE. Oh. I'm sorry, Shelly, that didn't occur to me. Is it all right? I thought as long as we're committed to the trip we ought to try to make it as good as possible.

MARY-ELLEN. You want us to pay you for the extra dose?

ROBBIE. Hey, what's the matter with everyone? Dane has had a very excellent good idea which I think we all oughta throw our support behind. O.K.?

SHELLY. If I was their guest I'd at least ask . . .

BILL. Shut up, baby.

ROBBIE. It's great how we're all getting off on each other. If there were a few more guns in the house we could shoot it out.

SHELLY. Forget it. I'm just weirded out by everyone being sick when I'm feeling O.K.

BILL. If there were some way we could share our sickness with you we'd do everything in our power. Don't baby. That's enough.

DANE. I also got ice cream, that's the other thing. I figured part of our sickness was because of the taste of the buttons, so the ice cream might help to mask it. You know.

ROBBIE. Yeeeech, ice cream.

DANE. Peppermint chip. Peppermint's very strong.

SHELLY. Why don't all you guys just have one big communal puke and get it over with.

MARY-ELLEN. I hope the trip at the end of this is worth the getting there.

SHELLY. The trip is in your head.

MARY-ELLEN. Shelly, can we do something later.

SHELLY. What do you mean?

MARY-ELLEN. I feel there's some kind of negative energy between us. I don't know exactly what it is but I feel it very strongly and it's gonna get in the way of a good event today if we don't do something about it, and just generally you know, bad vibes ought to be avoided because they're an outside force and you don't want to be controlled by an outside force. What I want to suggest is that when we're more into the high maybe we could concentrate on finding some good energy inside of us and we could work at directing that good energy towards each other, and then later we'll be able to refer back to that energy whenever we feel bad vibes developing between us.

DANE. Mary-Ellen's doing a lot of confrontation work.

SHELLY. I haven't got a single negative feeling about

you. Not one. I feel completely, positively wonderful about you.

MARY-ELLEN. I don't feel that's true. (SHELLY *looks helplessly at the others.*)

DANE. Why don't you two work that out later.

MARY-ELLEN. (*Emphatically to* SHELLY.) All right?

SHELLY. Sure. Fine.

BILL. The ice-cream's melting.

(*All are glad for a chance to break and get into something physical, like eating more of the stuff that created the situation from which they were glad to break and get into something physical, like eating more of the stuff . . . eat in relative silence. Some faces.* DANE *talks as he eats.*)

DANE. Five months ago. Less. On this mountain. Me and Mary-Ellen hiked to the top and took acid. What a strange trip that was. The sounds you can hear on acid, just lying there naked on our backs. We were naked, you see. We took all our clothes off. Except our socks. Leaves. Breezes. You could hear the sun moving through the sky. Whhsssh. And roots moving through the ground under your head. Insects. Ants all over our bodies. Thousands of ants, thousands of tiny legs running all over us. I sort of freaked out. I was terrified. Mary-Ellen couldn't feel them. Well, there weren't any, you see, I was just imagining it and anyway, Mary-Ellen was dancing. But this friend of mine had told me about a time when she'd been stoned on top of a mountain, a different mountain and she'd woken up with ants in her hair and her eyes and in her ears and crawling around her crotch and I just flipped out and everything in my body came out. I was urinating and defecating and crying and my nose was running and I was sweating and I felt so Christ-awful alone way on top of that mountain with nothing above us except sky and just a mountain underneath us, which isn't very much. Trapped in between. Mary-Ellen didn't seem to notice. She was rubbing against trees. It got better.

MARY-ELLEN. I remember. I was being a grizzly bear.

ROBBIE. Oh God, this ice cream, this ice cream, it's so green and so runny and it tastes so weird. It's like they didn't even bother to mix the chemicals together. I swear I can taste every single chemical separately. Green. Oh, I love it. It's so Twentieth Century. I would defend this ice cream against attack.

(SHELLY *begins to move in a kind of rhythm, dancing to music she hears in her head, very funky.*)

SHELLY. Come on, baby, let's dance.

BILL. Stop it, Shelly.

SHELLY. Please dance with me.

BILL. Cut it out. (SHELLY *moves off and dances on her own.*)

DANE. I'll dance with you, Shelly.

BILL. Cut the shit, Shelly.

ROBBIE. What's the matter with you, Billy-boy?

SHELLY. (*To herself.*) Ohhh, it's soooo good, it's sooo good. (BILL *gets up, takes the rifle.* DANE *grabs it from him.*)

DANE. Hey, man, take it easy. What are you doing? (BILL *looks at him blankly.*)

BILL. I'm going inside. How does that strike you? (BILL *takes the rifle back and exits indoors. Immediately,* SHELLY *goes in after him. Pause.*)

ROBBIE. Nice to see you guys. Nice of you to drop by.

DANE. You have some weird friends.

ROBBIE. Oh, Bill's just . . . he's like that sometimes. Life is a freak show, right?

DANE. (*Seriously.*) That depends really on how you look at it. (ROBBIE *bursts out laughing.*)

ROBBIE. You're the fucking limit. Hey, thanks for coming. (*He hugs* DANE *warmly.* DANE *returns the gesture but awkwardly.*)

MARY-ELLEN. We missed you.

ROBBIE. So, what do we all feel about life at this point in time?

MARY-ELLEN. Honey, why don't you take the ice cream back before it melts?

DANE. O.K. You could say leave me and Rob alone, you know.

MARY-ELLEN. Leave me and Robbie alone.

DANE. Yes. All right. I'll be inside. (*He exits inside with the cutting board.*)

ROBBIE. How'd you find out where I was? Did I leave clues?

MARY-ELLEN. Where are you going after this?

ROBBIE. I haven't thought about it. Maybe I'll stay, settle down, who knows? Countryside, ocean, and there's this check-out girl in Safeways. I mean, why not? What more could a man ask for? A wife, a life, a little bit of strife. Look, I enjoy moving around right now, O.K.?

MARY-ELLEN. I don't know. Is it?

ROBBIE. Sure, the call of the highway, new horizons, adventure, old friends, laughing, good times, saying hi.

MARY-ELLEN. I worry about you.

ROBBIE. Well don't. I'm fine.

MARY-ELLEN. Are you?

ROBBIE. Lay off, Mary.

MARY-ELLEN. I realized after you left . . . we'd never really talked. A whole month with us and I never learned anything about you. My husband's best friend.

ROBBIE. What? Is that what he said? I mean, sure, we went to school together but I always thought . . . well, it was more you and me. Sort of. You know.

MARY-ELLEN. I know. Why did you leave so suddenly. I was really upset.

ROBBIE. Oh, I don't know. I thought it was time to go. (*Pause.*) What do you want, Mary?

MARY-ELLEN. I want to know what's going on with you. How you're feeling.

ROBBIE. You came all the way up here today to find out how I was feeling?

MARY-ELLEN. Just talk to me, that's all. I've been thinking about you.

ROBBIE. What if I don't want to talk? What if I don't really want you to know me? What if I want to guard the big secret? Stay mysterious, elusive. What would you say to that?

MARY-ELLEN. I just want to be able to think about you in a certain way. I want to feel good about you. You remember the day you and me and Dane went to that park and . . .

ROBBIE. No. (*Deliberate.*) I don't. Look, Mary, whatever it is we could say to each other, the thing is, afterwards you'd go back to Dane and have dinner and talk and live your life . . . and that's very nice for you . . . and Dane . . . and I'm very happy for both of you. And I would just move on to some place else. Which is very nice for me. But it's different. Things are just a certain way, and the way they are is that we can't do anything about what both of us think it might be nice to do something about. And anyway, it wouldn't be very nice.

MARY-ELLEN. Hold my hand. It's all right.

ROBBIE. Oh, God, you get things so mixed up sometimes.

MARY-ELLEN. No I don't. Tell me what you're really thinking.

ROBBIE. I just fucking did. Tit.

MARY-ELLEN. What?

ROBBIE. Tit. Teat. Bosom. Breast. That's what I was really thinking, O.K.? Being suckled at your breast. May I do that?

MARY-ELLEN. Of course not.

ROBBIE. (*Laughing.*) And you want me to trust you?

MARY-ELLEN. Stop being like this, Rob.

ROBBIE. Like what? I just told you exactly what was going on in my mind. I had this very simple, straightforward urge to be suckled at the breast of my best friend's wife, in that way that friends do. End of conversation. Next question.

MARY-ELLEN. All right. Go ahead.

ROBBIE. Let's talk about something else, Mary.

MARY-ELLEN. God, you're the loneliest person I've ever met.

ROBBIE. Fuck off, Mary, just fuck off. Leave me alone. I haven't done anything to you. (*Calmer.*) Golly. Nice sun. For a while there I didn't think it was going to come out today. (*Pause.*) See, there's no point. (*Enter* REILLY *from around the corner. He's about forty-five or so. He clears his throat.*) Ah, Reilly, you old son of a gun, just in the nick of time. How the hell are you?

REILLY. Can't complain, can't complain.

ROBBIE. This is Mary-Ellen. Mary-Ellen, Reilly.

MARY-ELLEN. Hi.

REILLY. You found yourself a friend, eh?

ROBBIE. Yes, yes indeed. How is the missus?

REILLY. She's well, she's well.

ROBBIE. Good. I'm glad to hear it.

REILLY. Yes, she's doing fine.

ROBBIE. Great. Everyone's sort of . . . ah . . . inside. I'll tell them you're here.

REILLY. Could I trouble you for a glass of water? Just a glass of water, if you could manage, that is, if it's no trouble.

ROBBIE. Sure. Come on inside.

REILLY. I'll stay out here if it's all right with you. Just a glass of water. (*Enter Dane.*)

DANE. Whew, boy, I think that last batch must've done the trick. I'm getting incredible rushes.

ROBBIE. Dane, listen, this is Reilly. He's, ah. We're

just now in the process of. Jesus, this is pretty complicated. Inside my head, I mean. Reilly, fix on Reilly. We're buying a boat from Reilly. Well, we're considering. It's a fishing boat. We're going to fish. Commercially. Me and Bill. I didn't tell you that. This is, oh, Reilly, this is Dane.

DANE. You look exactly like a picture of my grandfather.

REILLY. That a fact? Well, I could do with a glass of water. I could use that.

ROBBIE. Sure. Whew. Some shit! (*He exits into house.*)

REILLY. Little something to wash down the pills. Got these little red ones here for the headache.

DANE. You get migraines?

REILLY. Couldn't get far without the red ones. The green ones I don't know. They're supposed to make you sleep better. I just about forgotten what the hell sleep is, you know. Oh, I take 'em, but. Total bitch in a ditch this pain business. Never mind. Never mind, hell, don't you pay any attention to me. Shit, I'm all right. I'll be fine. Don't believe I caught your name.

DANE. Dane.

REILLY. Dane, that's it! I remember now. Sure, Dane. I forgot the first time, that's what happened. Goes in here, comes out here. (*Ear to ear.*) Concentration's shot. It's a humiliating thing what pain does to you. When it keeps going on, I mean. Dane, that's it, got it now. Like a great Dane. That's the way to remember it. Great Dane.

MARY-ELLEN. Look at how the trees keep shifting colors. It's incredible. Did you bring the camera?

DANE. (*He mimes a camera.*) Click, got it.

MARY-ELLEN. Wow, pictures. Get one with me and Reilly over by the trees.

REILLY. Beg your pardon?

DANE. Woops.

MARY-ELLEN. (*Explaining.*) We just . . . ah . . .

DANE. Oh, have you met my wife Mary-Ellen?

REILLY. How do you do? Your wife. I thought you were friends with whatsit. Paul.

MARY-ELLEN. Rob.

REILLY. Oh Christ, my head, my head. (*He presses his hands over his eyes.*)

MARY-ELLEN. Dane, do something. He's in pain, Dane. (DANE *giggles.*) Dane!

DANE. (*Laughing.*) I'm sorry, honey, I can't help it. It was just how you said that. I can't stop, I'm sorry. (REILLY *recovers.*)

MARY-ELLEN. Hey, are you all right?

REILLY. I think it's over. Yeah, better, better. It comes in spurts like that. Comes and goes. Jesus, I wish to hell I was dead and that's the truth. Much better now, thank you. Just waiting for the water.

MARY-ELLEN. (*To* DANE.) You make me sick, Dane.

DANE. Hey-hey. I'm sorry. I couldn't control it. (*He hugs her.* MARY-ELLEN *exits into house.*)

REILLY. I guess we're in for a spell of good weather. Fellow at the Coast Guard said a few weeks of sun. Warm up the water. That's good for the silver. Yep, silvers are on top, you see, right near the surface. Fifty degrees and they bite. Funny thing about that. See, your Chinook stay right close to the bottom and your Silvers stay on top. Both of 'em salmon, but I don't suppose they ever even see each other. Figure that. You ever done any fishing there, Dane?

DANE. Fish talk to each other. Each species is supposed to have its own separate language and it can't be understood by any fish that isn't the same species. There's even supposed to be dialects. Complete sub-languages. Like up in Manitoba there's these bass that talk more like trout than . . . wait, it's not bass . . . it's pickerel . . . bass or pickerel . . . ?

REILLY. Oh, hell, yeah, there's all kinds of fish, that's true enough. Now, fish don't feel anything, there's an interesting fact while we're on information. Think of that. No such thing as a migraine in a fish. (*Enter* ROBBIE.)

ROBBIE. Hey, I can't find them anywhere.

(*Enter* BILL *and* SHELLY, *in a hurry*.)

BILL. Hey, Reilly, we just saw your car coming off the highway.

SHELLY. I'll make some hibiscus tea. Would you like some tea, Reilly

REILLY. I'll just have some water, if it's no trouble.

ROBBIE. Water! That was it. Sorry, Reilly. (SHELLY *exits inside*.)

REILLY. Just for the red pills, you see. What do you say, boys? Gonna catch yourself some fish?

BILL. Sure, why not?

REILLY. That's what I like to hear. Just got a new coat of paint on her. Looks real sweet. Don't know as I ought to sell her even.

BILL. Well, we're definitely interested.

ROBBIE. We're sort of wondering why she sank three times last winter.

REILLY. What's that?

ROBBIE. And why you never mentioned it.

BILL. (*To* ROBBIE.) You fuck.

REILLY. Now let me tell you boys a thing or two about last winter. That boat . . . the third time I didn't have nothing to do with it. And them first two times neither. Goddamn son of a bitch fool kid I hired to look after it. Shit, he didn't know a boat from a shoe full of snot. Hippie jackass is what he was. Up from California. Shit. I told him a thing or two. (REILLY *has another attack in his head*.) Damnit to holy fuck.

(ROBBIE *makes a move towards* REILLY *but* BILL *restrains him, watching in fascination*. REILLY *blacks out*.)

ROBBIE. He's dead.

BILL. (*He goes over to him.*) Hey, Reilly. (*He shakes him.* REILLY *stirs. Sits bolt upright.*)

REILLY. Where the hell am I? Oh. Jeeesus. How you boys doing? Could you get me a glass of water, could you? (*Enter* MARY-ELLEN *with a glass of water.* SHELLY *behind her.*)

MARY-ELLEN. Here you are, Reilly.

REILLY. Ah, you're a darling . . . ah . . .

MARY-ELLEN. Mary-Ellen.

REILLY. I appreciate it. (MARY-ELLEN *exits inside with* SHELLY. REILLY *takes his pills.*) Ah, that's better. That'll do it. Yes, sir, it's a good little boat. I started up that engine this morning and she purred like a kitten. All new valves. All new exhaust. Yeah, she's a good boat. You boys have a good think on it and I'll be around first thing tomorrow morning. First thing. (*Rises.*) You can't go wrong. Lick of paint. I'll tell you. I'm not feeling too hot. No. Take it easy. (*He exits around the house.*)

ROBBIE. You drive a hard bargain, sonny.

DANE. (*He has been watching from the side.*) He's in bad shape.

ROBBIE. He's gonna be stone dead a long time before we ever lay our hands on a thousand dollars.

REILLY. (*He re-enters.*) Say ah . . . oh, it's in the car. Can't keep track of paper. Take it easy. (*He re-exits.* BILL *follows. Stops.*)

BILL. He's dying. Rory's right. The guy's dying. He's standing here talking to us and he's dying. How can he do that?

ROBBIE. So, what's wrong with dying?

BILL. No, I mean how can the guy just be walking around like that when he's dying? It's fucking evil.

(*Car engine starts Offstage. Car leaving.*)

ROBBIE. What do you want to play now?

DANE. I have a frisbee in the Volvo. Should I get it?

ROBBIE. Yeah, get the frisbee.

DANE. It's in the Volvo. I'll get it. (*Pause.*) I'll be right back. (*He exits.*)

ROBBIE. Hey.

BILL. What?

ROBBIE. Where's Dane?

(*They laugh. Enter* SHELLY *and* MARY-ELLEN. MARY-ELLEN *is laughing hysterically. She has a pot on her head like a helmet.*)

MARY-ELLEN. Hey, look at me. What do I have on my head?

BILL. A pot.

MARY-ELLEN. I'm a pothead. (*All laugh hysterically. They stop.* MARY-ELLEN *takes the pot off.*) Where's Dane? (BILL *and* ROBBIE *bust up.*)

ROBBIE. He's getting the frisbee from the Volvo.

MARY-ELLEN. The frisbee? Why?

ROBBIE. He wanted to.

BILL. We told him it was all right. (*This is giggly. Enter* DANE *with the frisbee.*)

DANE. What's going on? (*They laugh. Can't explain.*)

SHELLY. Hey, is this really as funny as I think it is?

BILL. I'm not feeling nauseous any more.

ROBBIE. Do you . . . realize what this means . . . doctor?

ALL. WE'RE STONED . . .

ROBBIE. Again! (*They all cheer. Light changes to somber, dark, to suggest a cloud passing over the sun. All stop.*)

MARY-ELLEN. What was that?

DANE. Look. (*They all look towards the mountain.*)

MARY-ELLEN. Holy Jesus. Look at it.

ROBBIE. It's a pretty tacky effect, don't you think? No, I think it's very beautiful. Why? Well, I've never seen fog rolling over a mountain top like that. Oh, well, it happens all the time here. That's fascinating. Yes, we like it. Shall I go on? No. O.K.

SHELLY. That's gotta be a miracle. Can we go to the lookout?

BILL. Sure.

DANE. What's the lookout?

SHELLY. It's this place over the ocean. It's incredible in the fog.

MARY-ELLEN. Oh, wow, yes, let's go there. (*General assent.*)

DANE. We'll take the Volvo.

SHELLY. Far out.

ROBBIE. (*To* BILL.) You got the keys to the cycle?

BILL. Sure.

SHELLY. Don't be a party-pooper. Come in the nifty red Volvo.

ROBBIE. I'll take the cycle.

BILL. Shelly, baby, it's cool on the cycle.

MARY-ELLEN. Are you sure it's safe? I mean, the fog. Why don't you come in the car?

ROBBIE. Jesus, would you please stop making a fuss. Give me the keys.

DANE. (*Weird.*) You should make up your mind if you want us to be worried about you or not.

MARY-ELLEN. Dane!

ROBBIE. (*He does a mock baby cry.*) You're not supposed to notice that, Dane, and if you do notice it you're not supposed to say anything, and if you do say anything it's supposed to be a joke. (*He exits with keys.*)

BILL. Hey, follow our lights.

DANE. Let's go. (*He and* MARY-ELLEN *exit.*)

SHELLY. Hey, what happened to Reilly?

BILL. He went home.

SHELLY. Well? Are we fisherfolk?

BILL. It's weird.

SHELLY. Is everything cool?

BILL. You mean like all around.

SHELLY. Yeah. You know.

BILL. Isn't it always?

DANE. (*He calls from Offstage.*) Hey, let's go.

SHELLY. (*Imitating.*) Hey, let's go. (*They exit arm in arm.*)

END ACT ONE

ACT TWO

SCENE 1

"The lookout." A ledge of rock bordered by a wire fence with a run of barbed wire on top. A lighthouse just visible at the side. Its rotating light illuminates the Stage every forty-five seconds. There's a set of binoculars on a rotating stand that you pay a dime to look through. It's fogged in. The actors can't see each other more than five feet away. No special effects, just acting. Everything has a slow quality about it. They are all in a private mood, the way you get on peyote in the fog. The Volvo is parked on stage. So is the cycle, a Norton Atlas, 1969.

At the start, this: BILL *is looking through the binoculars.* SHELLY *sits huddled against the fence.* MARY-ELLEN *looks out at the ocean. Slow, distant waves, below.* ROBBIE *and* DANE *are conducting an experiment in visibility.* DANE *stands still while* ROBBIE *backs slowly away.*

DANE. Further. Further. Further. There.

ROBBIE. No, I can still see you.

DANE. (*Peering.*) Oh yes. O.K. A little more.

ROBBIE. (*He goes back further.*) There! I can't see you now. Stand still and I'll pace it off.

DANE. No, you stay there. I know my shoe size exactly.

ROBBIE. So do I. Nine D.

DANE. You have to know the inches. Mine are exactly ten and three-eighths from toe to the heel.

ROBBIE. I hope I'm having a good time.

DANE. I'm coming. (ROBBIE *feints back and circles around the vehicles to* SHELLY *while* DANE *paces his*

36

way Offstage. Exiting.) Boy, distances are really deceptive in the fog. (ROBBIE *settles down by* SHELLY.)

SHELLY. Wouldn't it be far out if you were a bird and you could just fly through the fog, nothing on any side of you, just fog?

ROBBIE. With my luck I'd crash into the lighthouse. (*The light pulses. They look up.*)

SHELLY. It's so incredibly beautiful.

ROBBIE. I don't know. I can't see anything.

DANE. (*Offstage.*) Hey, Rob!

ROBBIE. Over here.

DANE. (*Offstage.*) You shithead!

ROBBIE. Dane? Dane? Come in, Dane. I've lost radio contact. Commander . . . there's something sinister about this planet. I don't know what it is but . . . yes, yes, I understand what it is that's making the hair stand up straight on the back of my head, Commander . . . the spatial relations are all wrong. Straight lines are . . . curved. All facts are untrue here. There's nothing to grab hold of. Dane. Come in, Dane, come in. (MARY-ELLEN *turns from the fence and begins acting like an alien life form with antennae. She makes weird noises.*) Do you hear something weird, Varga? Something sinister in the fog?

SHELLY. I'm just into being . . . still.

ROBBIE. It's got you in its power, Shelly. It's dulling your mind. I feel like I've been drugged.

MARY-ELLEN. (*She finds her way to them.*) Beep-beep-beep. Hello . . . earthling . . . beep-beep. What . . . brings . . . you . . . to . . . our . . . pranet . . . beep . . . planet?

ROBBIE. I am looking for my colleague, Commander Dane . . . can you help me?

MARY-ELLEN. Do . . . you . . . really . . . want . . . my . . . hep . . . beep . . . help . . . beep . . . beep . . . I . . . mean . . . really?

ROBBIE. Yes, o strange little alien life form. Give me a message I can bring back to earth.

MARY-ELLEN. Listen . . . carefully . . . earthling.

ROBBIE. Yes? Yes? What?

MARY-ELLEN. I . . . love . . . you . . . beep. (*She turns abruptly and goes away, still being a spaceman.* ROBBIE *makes a slight involuntary gesture towards her.* DANE *appears at the edge of the stage.*)

DANE. Rob? Mary-Ellen? (MARY-ELLEN *goes to the Volvo, gets in and honks the horn, a long, loud honk.* DANE *runs to the window and knocks. Tries the door. It's locked.*) Mary-Ellen. MARY-ELLEN, OPEN THE DOOR. SHE'S LOCKED HERSELF IN.

MARY-ELLEN. (*She opens the door and comes out as a spaceman.*) Herro . . . Hello . . . earthling. Do . . . you . . . like . . . my . . . Volvo?

DANE. You're wearing the battery down, Mary-Ellen. Let's play frisbee.

MARY-ELLEN. I . . . love . . . you . . . earthling . . . (*She turns and exits, still as spaceman.*)

SHELLY. Boy, does she get on my tits.

ROBBIE. She's a friend of mine. A really good friend.

SHELLY. I'm trying, Rob, I really am. But she's just one of those people that gets on my tits. There aren't many, but when they do, they really do. My uncle was like that.

DANE. (*He gets the frisbee out of the car.*) I think it might be a lot of fun to play frisbee in the fog. Would anybody like to play frisbee?

ROBBIE. No, Dane.

SHELLY. No.

BILL. No.

(DANE *tosses it up and catches it. Starts to put it back in the car, changes his mind. He finds his way to* BILL.)

DANE. Can you see anything?

BILL. Yeah. (DANE *watches him, looks at the fog.*)

DANE. The lighthouse flashes exactly once every

forty-five seconds. (BILL *continues to look through the binoculars.*)

SHELLY. What does the fog make you think of?

ROBBIE. Death.

SHELLY. Really?

ROBBIE. Yes. Or life. In that area.

SHELLY. I had a flash that we were on this giant movie set. The fog was just a veil, or something, and if it lifted suddenly we'd see these banks of lights on us and movie cameras and God would be sitting in one of those chairs with his name on it, Director, Mr. God, and he'd be yelling cut, cut, do the whole thing again.

ROBBIE. Oh, I hope so . . .

SHELLY. What?

ROBBIE. . . . that we can do the whole thing . . . (*Stopping.*) Never mind.

SHELLY. You know, I have regular contact with the dead.

BILL. You want to have a look?

DANE. I don't understand how you can see anything in the fog.

BILL. You have to put a dime in. (BILL *does.* DANE *looks.*)

ROBBIE. No, I didn't know that.

SHELLY. I've been talking to King Solomon for two years.

ROBBIE. How's he doing?

SHELLY. I know this sounds weird. That's why I never tell anyone.

ROBBIE. Shelly? Shelly-friend? Shelly-Bill's-Old-Lady? Hello?

SHELLY. He's been explaining why you shouldn't be afraid of death, because it doesn't stop there. You keep going onto higher forms of energy, until . . . I don't know. I can't understand him when he starts that rap. But you're not supposed to take life. It makes it harder for you to move up to the next state of energy after you die. That's where "Thou shalt not kill" comes from.

ROBBIE. Oh, that's where.

SHELLY. According to him. (*Back to* DANE *and* BILL.)

DANE. I can't see anything.

BILL. You don't see the fog?

DANE. Of course I can see the fog.

BILL. Just look at it and let the images come to you. It's like a screen. If you don't want to do it . . .

DANE. Oh, I see. Let me try that. (ROB *and* SHELLY.)

SHELLY. This is between us, O.K.?

ROBBIE. Bill doesn't know?

SHELLY. I get so worried about the way he gets violent. If he'd killed Guinevere.

ROBBIE. Ah. You did put the egg there.

SHELLY. Don't tell him.

ROBBIE. He wouldn't kill Guinevere.

SHELLY. Last year, when we had the farm, he killed our cow. Shot it in the face.

ROBBIE. Bill did?

SHELLY. He said it wasn't giving enough milk.

ROBBIE. Oh, no wonder.

SHELLY. Why, what kind of a person did you think I was?

ROBBIE. What?

SHELLY. Didn't you just say . . . oh. I'm so stoned. I love this stuff.

ROBBIE. The other day I went in the bathroom right after you'd been there was the most amazing turd I've ever seen lurking at the bottom of the toilet. I was just completely overcome with awe at the sight of this perfectly formed solitary turd and all I could think was, that's Shelly for ya. Down to earth. Calm. Complete. I'm just . . . you asked what kind of person I thought you were. You don't mind my talking to you like this, turd to turd.

SHELLY. You want to know something amazing? I remember that. Last week.

ROBBIE. Yeah.

SHELLY. Well. That wasn't mine. It was Bills, and I had exactly the same thought except just the opposite. I couldn't figure out how he could be so violent and have such a calm turd. I'm not calm at all, you know.

ROBBIE. I really like you, Shelly.

SHELLY. (*She lays her head on his shoulder.*) I feel sad.

ROBBIE. You mean just now? Or always. And why?

SHELLY. Oh shit.

MARY-ELLEN. (*She enters as a spaceman.*) Where . . . is . . . everyone . . . beep . . . beep. (*She finds* DANE.)

DANE. This is incredible. You should try this, Mary-Ellen.

MARY-ELLEN. What . . . do . . . you . . . see . . . out . . . there . . . beep . . . beep.

DANE. You can project perfect visual images onto the fog. There's some chemical in this peyote that activates the optical centers or something. It's like watching your own movie.

MARY-ELLEN. Beep . . . beep . . . far . . . out . . . goodbye . . . (MARY-ELLEN *goes to* SHELLY *and* ROB.) Hello . . . Rob . . . beep . . . hello . . . Shelly . . . beep . . . beep . . . do . . . I . . . get . . . on . . . your . . . tits . . . Shelly? (*Pause.*) Beep.

SHELLY. (*She gets up suddenly.*) Would you please leave me alone.

MARY-ELLEN. Beep . . . beep . . . I . . . do . . . not . . . understand . . . your . . . request. Beep. Please . . . go . . . deeper. Beeper.

SHELLY. Because I'm not into it, O.K.? Do it, but leave me out.

MARY-ELLEN. Still . . . not . . . connecting. Beep. Please . . . go deeper . . . beeper. (SHELLY *screams. This turns to a kind of hysterical laugh.*)

SHELLY. You're crazy, you know that. You're completely god-damned crazy.

MARY-ELLEN. I . . . know . . . beep beep . . . I've . . . had . . . analysis. (*Straight.*) I can't understand why you don't like me, Shelly. Please like me.

ROBBIE. Will you please like her. She's my friend, Shelly.

SHELLY. (*She goes to* BILL.) I want to go for a walk.

BILL. Have a nice time.

SHELLY. Will you come with me?

BILL. No.

SHELLY. Please.

BILL. No.

SHELLY. Why not?

BILL. I don't feel like it.

DANE. I'll go for a walk with you.

SHELLY. I don't want to go with you. I mean . . . thanks, but I want to go with Bill.

BILL. And I don't want to go.

SHELLY. Bill!!! Who wants to go for a walk?

MARY-ELLEN. Me me me me me me . . . (MARY-ELLEN *and* ROBBIE *exchange smiles.*)

SHELLY. Oh fuck it. Come on, let's go. Where are you? (MARY-ELLEN *and* SHELLY *go for a walk.*)

ROBBIE. (*Apart.*) The fog's getting thinner. I can see you guys' outline. (BILL *watches* DANE *looking through the binoculars. A pause.*)

BILL. What's architecture like?

DANE. Huh?

BILL. You're an architect, right?

DANE. Yeah, I'm an architect.

BILL. What's it like. You like it. I mean, I bet it's a good job, being an architect. You seem pretty . . . like someone with a good job.

DANE. It's O.K. In fact, I like the actual work very much, and I like the people I work with. And a lot of jobs get created as a result of the work we do, which isn't the most important thing, but it's good to know. I guess some people don't care so much but

I really like having a good income, you know, being able to think about the future, plan things, give my kids a good education, take care of my folks when they're older . . . Mary-Ellen's folks. Oh, I remember now, the really incredible thing about architecture, and I just realized this the other day, it's something about the structures you work with, I mean the way you have to train yourself to think about your materials from the point of view of an underlying structure, it means that you're always looking for the order behind things, and when you apply that kind of thinking to the whole world, you find that everything becomes clearer and clearer all the time, everything makes more and more sense, you know, falls into certain patterns, like a sort of design that you can keep filling in as you learn things. I mean I didn't know that I'd think about things that way when I was studying architecture. It just happened, and then the other day I realized that I'd had a kind of perfect accident happen to me. . . . I had this work that would always illuminate things about the world for me. I don't know, maybe a lot of people feel that way about their work. Oh, that's not what you asked, is it? I guess I got carried away. What did you ask?

BILL. Let me see your frisbee. (DANE *gives it over abstractly*.) Don't you want to play, Dane?

DANE. I just want to look through here a little more. I'll be with you in a little while.

BILL. (*He goes near* ROBBIE.) Hey, Cisco. Looks like you and me.

ROBBIE. (*Turns*.) Yeah, right, sheet! (*Spits*.)

BILL. Sheet! (*Spits*.)

ROBBIE. (*He backs up towards the fence and holds up his pinkie*.) On the pinkie. . . . (BILL *throws. The frisbee sails over the fence into the ocean*.) Woops.

BILL. Woops? Oh. Um. I wonder if Dane's got another frisbee.

(BILL *and* ROBBIE *lean up against the fence looking out onto the ocean, fingers clutching the wire.*)

ROBBIE. Bill, Bill, we've lost the frisbee.

BILL. Frisbee gone to great waters to join Father Frisbee.

DANE. This is just absolutely amazing. I mean, I just wouldn't have believed this is possible. (DANE *doesn't seem to be speaking to anyone, but he's intense.*)

BILL. You got some weird friends.

ROBBIE. Yeah, they kill cows and stuff.

BILL. What's amazing, Dane?

DANE. Out there. No, wait a minute. I guess I mean "in here."

BILL. It must be really quiet, down there.

ROBBIE. Do you really want to go through with this boat thing?

BILL. No, asshole, I just moved out here for my fucking health. Look, if you want out, just say and I'll get Larry or Ed Nolin to come in with me. There's hundreds of guys that want to have a boat.

ROBBIE. I just asked.

BILL. Well I just answered. (ROBBIE *takes an envelope out of his pocket and hands it to* BILL. BILL *opens it. It's money.*) What the fuck is this?

ROBBIE. It's fifteen hundred dollars in denominations of one hundred.

BILL. Where's this from?

ROBBIE. My rich daddy.

BILL. When did this happen?

ROBBIE. I've had it for a while. I just wanted to be sure you were for real about the boat.

BILL. Me? What about you.

ROBBIE. Well. Strictly speaking . . . to keep the record accurate it isn't a sort of life or death affair for me, salmon fishing. I'm very used to living off pa. In fact, I've reached a point where I honestly get deep pleasure spending his money. Not in a bitter, spiteful, hatefilled, self-destructive way. I feel generous and wise and even helpful as I spread it around. He doesn't really know how to enjoy it, and I do. And in the long run, which is the only run that counts, he's going to die and you're going to die and the earth is going to crumble into dust, when the sun burns out, at least that's what I've been told, so what the fuck. And, of course, I adore the sea.

BILL. Hang on. I appreciate this, man. I really do. But why didn't you let me know you had the bread? I mean I've been busting my ass trying to figure out a way to get a hold of that boat and you've been holding onto all this bread, am I for real, what kind of bullshit game is that?

ROBBIE. You haven't been busting your ass, Bill. You've been thinking about it, sure, sort of, maybe even a whole lot, sure, kind of. Listen, I like you, man, I really like you a lot, but I see you. I can't help it. I see the game, what you're doing. The farm. The trucking business. The pot plantation in Brazil. What else? A million beautiful trips, Billy. But someone or something always fucked you over. The shits out there always beat you back. Well, what happens if the great salmon enterprise fails; some other great shit comes along and dumps on you only this time, this time you don't get away with blaming it on everything around you. What happens if you realize the fucking up is built right into you like an extra liver, and you're gonna have to take it with you wherever you go. For the rest of your life? I don't want to finance a move that's gonna break you. You're thirty, man. It's starting to be really important.

BILL. Well, just who the holy fuck do you think you are, all of a sudden.

ROBBIE. Forget about me. I'm a rich son of a bitch with nothing to do. I drift around. I live off the friends I have. Oh, I pay, but it's not even my money. Look,

I've seen it, Billy. I know what I am and it's O.K., I'm indestructible. I live off your happiness. O.K. You're energy. I dig on the fact that things really matter to you, that you have lives. They do things. All my friends. See, I want you to do this thing, I want you to have a fleet of five hundred boats if that's what you want and I want your life to be good and I want you to be happy with your life and your Shelly and your chicken and . . .

BILL. You're spooky.

ROBBIE. Shit, I didn't mean to say any of that. It's not even true. I find most of my friends pathetic, including you. Take the fucking money. I conned it out of some weird old guy. He buys stocks in dog shit.

BILL. Rob. What's up.

ROBBIE. Take the money. I'm just talking. That's what I do.

BILL. (*Cheering.*) We're gonna get that fleet of five hundred boats, fuckhead, you and me. You wait and see. And one day just for the pure dumb hell of it I'm gonna line 'em up end to end and sail around the whole fucking planet with a stereo playing rock and roll and I'll be laughing so hard they'll hear it on Mars. Put that money in your pocket. We're going fishing.

ROBBIE. I don't trust myself with that much cash. You hold onto it.

BILL. (*Taking it.*) Hey man.

ROBBIE. What man.

BILL. You got an ugly soul.

ROBBIE. (*Laughing.*) Right, right.

(*They shake.* BILL *whoops for joy, yells, laughs, whatever.*)

BILL. We're going fishing, goddamn. We are going fishing. *All right.* Hey, Dane, you beautiful motherfucker, stoke up the Volvo, we're buying a boat. A BOAT. A fishing boat, man. And I'm gonna buy you two hundred and fifty new frisbees and a tank of gas and we'll have a Chinese meal and take more buttons and Holy Shit, man, it's all coming to-fucking-gether.

DANE. You want to go into town. (BILL *busts up and* DANE's *low-key reaction.*)

BILL. Oh Dane, Dane, Dane, you're so together.

DANE. You want to go right away is what I meant.

BILL. (*He gets mock calm-serious.*) See, the thing is, there's this fisherman Reilly . . . Oh, you met him. Well he has a boat, and we're gonna buy it. O.K. You drive us into town and you get to watch us sign the papers. I got the cash right here. Fifteen hundred buckeroos.

DANE. Well. We ought to get the girls.

BILL. Shelly! Shelly-Baby! We're buying a boat, wanna come.

DANE. Mary-Ellen!

BILL. Shelly. Mary-Ellen and Shelly.

MARY-ELLEN. Yoo-hoo. We're coming, don't go without us. (*They enter.*)

SHELLY. They're over here. (*During all this* ROBBIE *is climbing over the fence on the other side of the lookout.*) What's going on. What's this about a boat?

BILL. Shelly-baby-pie, we're getting us a boat. We got the money. Rob just put up fifteen hundred. He had it all along. Look.

SHELLY. Ahaaaa? Cripes. That's just . . . oh my god . . .

BILL. Yeah . . . ain't it just . . . (*They laugh hysterically.*)

MARY-ELLEN. Is this for the fishing thing? I thought both of you guys were doing it together.

BILL. Yeah, me and Rob.

MARY-ELLEN. Why did he give you the money?

BILL. Why did he give me the money? What difference does it make. You want to hold it.

MARY-ELLEN. (*Worried.*) Where's Rob?

BILL. He's here. What's the matter with you?

MARY-ELLEN. ROB? ROBBIE!! (*Silence.*)

DANE. Mary-Ellen, is something the matter?

MARY-ELLEN. ROBBIE!! (*Silence.* ROBBIE *is stuck on the fence.*)

ROBBIE. Tee-hee. I seem to be stuck over here. Or "help." (MARY-ELLEN *and others follow his voice. They go to him.*)

MARY-ELLEN. Rob? Are you all right?

ROBBIE. Hi gang. There's this frisbee down there. Anyone want to help.

BILL. That's a sort of shitty idea Rob cause that's an eighty-foot drop.

ROBBIE. I'll throw it up.

DANE. Put your hand on my shoulder. (*They help him down.*)

ROBBIE. Fuck it, we'll get a new frisbee.

BILL. Yeah, come on, we're going into town to get a boat.

SHELLY. Let's wait til tomorrow with the boat, O.K.?

ROBBIE. Strike while the iron's hot, that's what I say. I always say that. Always.

BILL. I'll follow you guys on the cycle.

ROBBIE. I'll take the cycle.

MARY-ELLEN. Rob.

SHELLY. You take the cycle, Rob. We'll meet you in town.

MARY-ELLEN. NO! I mean. For christ sakes everyone.

ROBBIE. Ah hah. I see. Oh oh oh. (*Laughing.*) No gang, I was not attempting to end it all. You stupid shits. A little self pity, O.K., but I want to be around to milk it.

BILL. (*Hands over keys.*) Meet us at Reilly's.

ROBBIE. Have a nice drive. (*He exits with cycle.*)
MARY-ELLEN. This is wrong.

(*Cycle engine starting, roaring off.*)

BILL. Who was that masked man?
SHELLY. Let's buy a boat.
MARY-ELLEN. We shouldn't've let him go. (SHELLY
gets in the car. BILL *too.*) Dane, you know him. He
was trying to kill himself.
DANE. Get in the Volvo, Mary-Ellen.
MARY-ELLEN. Why are you ignoring me?
DANE. Because there's only two things he can do.
He can either kill himself or not kill himself, and
either way, I don't care. (*Pause.*) I'm sorry. I just
went to school with him. I don't care. (DANE *gets in
the car.* MARY-ELLEN *alone. Car starts. Fade.*)

(*End* SCENE 1.)

ACT TWO

SCENE 2

Back to square one. The Living Room. DANE *is asleep
on the couch, his head on* MARY-ELLEN'S *lap.*
SHELLY *is curled up on the easy chair.* RORY *is on
a chair. Long pause.*

RORY. Whew. The end. I've seen a lot of dead dudes
in my day but I want to tell you that dude was dead.
I'll tell you the good news though. When it's funeral
time, they got a cosmetic guy in town that'll make that
bod look like Saturday night at the Roxy. It's a fucking miracle what they can do with cosmetics. Whew.
Really. It's an art.
SHELLY. I've never been . . . seen anyone dead up

close like that. I mean that I knew. It's such a waste. (SHELLY *cries*.)

MARY-ELLEN. Do you believe in God.

RORY. I do, man. I believe in everything.

SHELLY. It's just not the same as what you think. God, he was such a mess on the road. It didn't even look like a body.

RORY. Really. Death is the ultimate trip, right? Right!

SHELLY. Shut up, Rory.

RORY. Hey, babe, don't back into me, like my head is there, my mouth is there. Zip zip. That's how I am. I care. I'm feeling all kinds of stuff. I dug him. He was a truly far-out dude.

ROBBIE. (*He enters with a tray of coffee.*) Come and get it. What did Dane want? (*He sets the tray down. They help themselves.*)

MARY-ELLEN. He's out.

ROBBIE. Where'd Bill go.

SHELLY. He's taking a walk. You should see the stars out there. It's gonna be a nice day tomorrow.

ROBBIE. Do you think he's really cut up about Reilly.

SHELLY. I guess. He really dug that Reilly was a fisherman. You know.

ROBBIE. Yeah.

RORY. It's better this way. Fffft. Out like a fuse, nothing to lose. Blood clots are a bummer. My dad cashed in on a hemorrhage. One day. Twenty-two hours. Blubbering and pissing in the sheets. Messy scene. Didn't even recognize the kid til the last minute. Weird. Weird. You know what that old fucker said to me on the way out. Big exit line. Kid, he says, how come you're such a jerkoff? Man, what do you say to that? Know what I did? Springfield General Hospital. Into the men's room and jerk off. Really. Very heavy day. Oh, things can get so fucking beee-zare.

MARY-ELLEN. I don't think I like peyote.

Rory. Any of that shit left? Lay some on the kid for partytime?

Shelly. In the ice-box. I'm sorry we can't make it.

Rory. I'm hip, I'm hip. Be cool. Be mellow. Remember me in your dreams. Listen. We're putting Reilly in the turf in a few days. Don't know when yet but like he didn't have a whole lot of friends, you know? Just Mrs. Reilly.

Shelly. We'll be there.

Rory. Beautiful. Beautiful. (*Pause.*) It's such a fucking shame, ain't it? (*Nods and exits.*)

Robbie. They found his head a hundred feet away from the body.

Mary-Ellen. Even the last couple of acid trips haven't been all that great. I used to get off a lot more on tripping.

Shelly. Do you have any children.

Mary-Ellen. Not yet. We're not into . . . no.

Shelly. My body's falling apart. Just in little ways, but enough so you notice it. In the thighs. Around here. It has to happen sooner or later I guess. I'm sorry I don't like you more, Mary-Ellen. It's stupid.

Mary-Ellen. That's life.

Robbie. Hey, come on, come on, let's play a game or something. Put on some music. Play a game. Yuk it up.

Shelly. No.

Robbie. Is Dane asleep?

Mary-Ellen. Looks like it.

Robbie. Would you make sure. I want to tell you something.

Mary-Ellen. Danie. Arf-arf. Woof-woof. Frank Lloyd Wright! (*To* Robbie.) Well?

Robbie. (*Pause.*) Hey, let's go off some place together, us three. Canada. Start a commune.

Mary-Ellen. Rob.

Robbie. Up on the lookout before. I mean I guess it was obvious to the meanest of intelligences, but when I went off on the cycle, I really did intend as much as I ever intend anything, no more, much more . . . suicide.

MARY-ELLEN and SHELLY. I know. (*They exchange glances.*)

ROBBIE. Yes I know you know. I mean I know you knew what I wanted you to think, but I have a way of not being serious about things and I was *very* serious about . . . was it really that obvious?

SHELLY. You know it was.

ROBBIE. It felt so amazing in the fog. A hundred miles an hour. I could've had an accident before I had a chance to off myself. I was sort of scared but the scared went into just perfect peace. Perfect control. And I thought, O.K., do it. Just like that. All I need is a set of headlights. I went around this curve. Nothing. Still deserted. Then I started to feel kind of weird. Self-conscious. I mean, who was watching? Who was I doing this for? Who am I doing everything I'm doing for. I mean, are they watching? Who the fuck is this crowd that doesn't want me around? I mean this is pathetic, I'm going through this incredible performance and no one's watching. I was pissed off. And then I thought, wait a minute, I'm talking to myself. I'm out in the fog on a motorcycle travelling one hundred miles an hour with the intention of committing suicide and I'm talking to myself. And then suddenly it all stopped; the voices, the intention, the trip, the day, everything, and I saw something amazing inside of me that was so clear you could almost touch it with your finger . . . life: stay alive. I wanted like crazy to stay alive. Which means that, in balance, there must be something in it. Under all that bullshit one simple thing. Keep on. Stay alive. Pardon my being sincere for a moment. But I'm really glad I saw that. (*Long pause.*)

MARY-ELLEN. I guess we ought to be starting back.

We have a long drive. Dane. Dane, baby . . . (*She shakes him. He sits bolt upright.*)

DANE. Birds. Damn, it was birds. That's why I couldn't think of the kind of fish. It was birds. Bird calls. They have dialects, you see. Never mind.

MARY-ELLEN. We have to get going.

DANE. I'm getting so inaccurate. That's unforgiveable. Birds.

(BILL *enters with* GUINEVERE, *dead and plucked.*)

SHELLY. You didn't! Bill, Bill, Billy, why?

BILL. Cook it up. There'll be enough for all of us.

SHELLY. You're a bastard. And you're a failure. And you're pathetic. (SHELLY *goes off through the kitchen door.*)

BILL. Who's hungry?

DANE. What was that?

BILL. Nothing. This used to be Guinevere. She was a game we were playing.

MARY-ELLEN. We have to go. Thanks. Dane has to work tomorrow. Monday.

ROBBIE. It's Sunday. It's Sunday. That's what today is. It happens to be a very important fact.

BILL. Right. Sunday.

DANE. (*He rises.*) Well, Thank you very much.

MARY-ELLEN. (*She and* ROB *hug.*) Take care of yourself. Come have a suck one day.

ROBBIE. (*He goes to* DANE.) Thanks for dropping by. Happy building.

DANE. Good luck. That was excellent peyote. I enjoyed that. Say goodbye to Shelly. (*He exits with* MARY-ELLEN.)

ROBBIE. (*Spits.*) Well.

BILL. Sheet. (*Spits.*) Back to square one.

ROBBIE. What do you mean?

BILL. Looking for another boat.

ROBBIE. Isn't Reilly's still for sale?

BILL. You gotta be kidding. That's all I need. Ride around the high seas in a dead-man's boat. That'd be real cute.

ROBBIE. I didn't know you were superstitious.

BILL. The guy's a jinx. Look at the way he went out. His boat goes down three times at the dock and he gets splattered all over the highway. Stinking blood clots, One little wedge of red snot in his brain and . . . it's so stupid.

ROBBIE. Dying's dying.

BILL. The cop told me they found Reilly's head . . .

ROBBIE. I know.

BILL. He must've really been travelling.

ROBBIE. I guess.

BILL. It's weird. You'd think he'd've slowed down if he blacked out. Don't your muscles relax and you go limp.

ROBBIE. If Dane were here we could find out for sure.

BILL. Holy shit. That beautiful old fart. You know what that means?

ROBBIE. It means he's dead.

BILL. It means he killed himself. He went out on the highway and deliberately offed himself. He couldn't take the idea of walking around looking like such a mess so he did it himself.

ROBBIE. What difference does it make.

BILL. Oh asshole, can't you see anything? You think lying around in a hospital full of pills and rubber tubes and stink everywhere . . . you think that's the same as gracing out on a highway. This puts it right, what he did. We gotta have that boat, man. We gotta.

ROBBIE. Bill . . .

BILL. Don't sit there all calm on me, Robbie-boy. I can't spell this out in black and white but I know what I'm saying and I know it's right just the way I know everything is full of shit most of the time and

I don't know why it's full of shit and I can't write a
book about it for you but it's all gray . . . everything
in the middle . . . everyone's under shadows, under
rocks like a bunch of moles and all this totally ridic-
ulous stuff keeps happening to them and they just take
it and take it and take it and never raise a stink,
never fight back and Reilly did it. He saw what was
coming and he said No, man, fuck this, I don't have to
swallow this last piece of shit, don't say anything.
(BILL *in a rage kicks the couch that* ROBBIE *is on,
kicks other things, tears* GUINEVERE *apart.* ROBBIE
*rises calmly, goes to him and starts fighting mechan-
ically. It's a long, awful ritual.* ROBBIE *finally pins
him.* BILL *lies panting.*)

ROBBIE. Another day, another trip.

BILL. Oh, man, what the fuck is wrong with me?
How come you're always so calm.

ROBBIE. Good toilet training and a happy youth.

BILL. A lot of the time I feel like busting your
head open.

ROBBIE. I still wouldn't lay any eggs.

BILL. What? Oh. You ever had chicken stew?

ROBBIE. Dane's building a city. My buddy. Dane.
A whole new city someplace. Bolivia. Peru. One of
those places. If his idea is accepted there'll be this
whole new city someplace with people living their
lives in it and he designed it. Dane. The frisbee
champion of my high school.

BILL. Dane's an asshole.

ROBBIE. Yeah.

BILL. He's O.K.

ROBBIE. Yeah.

BILL. Fishing is a pretty dumb idea, isn't it.

ROBBIE. Yeah.

BILL. I mean, I've never even been on a boat before.
What if we get seasick. What if we sink. What if we
can't make a living. I mean, *I* can't. What if you de-
cide to take your money back.

ROBBIE. I won't.

BILL. You gonna stay out here.

ROBBIE. Yeah.

BILL. And fish.

ROBBIE. Sure.

BILL. Why?

ROBBIE. Cause it's something to do. Oh you're right, it's a dumb idea, no doubt about it. You and me. Two of the finest minds of our generation. But it's something to do. And, you know, if we approach it just the right way, after a while, if we manage to stick to it, and we don't get seasick and we do catch fish we might find there's a good reason for doing it.

BILL. Another trip.

ROBBIE. Fuck it, why not.

SHELLY. (*She enters.*) Give me Guinevere. I'll cook her.

BILL. Shelly-baby.

SHELLY. Don't talk to me. I'm tired and I'm upset.

BILL. I'm sorry.

SHELLY. I don't care. (*She exits with* GUINEVERE'S *corpse.* BILL *starts to follow. Turns.*)

BILL. Reilly's boat. First thing in the morning!

ROBBIE. I think maybe after the funeral.

BILL. Right. Right. (BILL *exits.*)

(ROBBIE *takes the .22, goes to the front door. He opens it. Aims at target outside. Fires.* BILL *rushes in.* ROBBIE *turns and smiles.*)

ROBBIE. Bull's-eye. (ROBBIE *leans the rifle against the wall and walks outside.* BILL *shakes his head and goes back into the kitchen. Watch the room for a moment. Blackout.*)

END

6 RMS RIV VU
BOB RANDALL

(Little Theatre) Comedy
4 Men, 4 Women, Interior

A vacant apartment with a river view is open for inspection by prospective tenants, and among them are a man and a woman who have never met before. They are the last to leave and, when they get ready to depart, they find that the door is locked and they are shut in. Since they are attractive young people, they find each other interesting and the fact that both are happily married adds to their delight of mutual, yet obviously separate interests.

> ". . . a Broadway comedy of fun and class, as cheerful as a rising souffle. A sprightly, happy comedy of charm and humor. Two people playing out a very vital game of love, an attractive fantasy with a precious tincture of truth to it."— *N.Y. Times.*
> ". . . perfectly charming entertainment, sexy, romantic and funny."—*Women's Wear Daily.*

Royalty, $50–$35

WHO KILLED SANTA CLAUS?
TERENCE FEELY

(All Groups) Thriller
6 Men, 2 Women, Interior

Barbara Love is a popular television 'auntie'. It is Christmas, and a number of men connected with her are coming to a party. Her secretary, Connie, is also there. Before they arrive she is threatened by a disguised voice on her Ansaphone, and is sent a grotesque 'murdered' doll in a coffin, wearing a dress resembling one of her own. She calls the police, and a handsome detective arrives. Shortly afterwards her guests follow. It becomes apparent that one of those guests is planning to kill her. Or is it the strange young man who turns up unexpectedly, claiming to belong to the publicity department, but unknown to any of the others?

> ". . . is a thriller with heaps of suspense, surprises, and nattily cleaver turns and twists . . . Mr. Feeley is technically highly skilled in the artificial range of operations, and his dialogue is brilliantly effective."—The Stage. London.

Royalty, $50–$25

VERONICA'S ROOM

IRA LEVIN

(Little Theatre) Mystery

2 Men, 2 Women, Interior

VERONICA'S ROOM is, in the words of one reviewer, "a chew-up-your-fingernails thriller-chiller" in which "reality and fantasy are entwined in a totally absorbing spider web of who's-doing-what-to-whom." The heroine of the play is 20-year-old Susan Kerner, a Boston University student who, while dining in a restaurant with Larry Eastwood, a young lawyer, is accosted by a charming elderly Irish couple, Maureen and John Mackey (played on Broadway by Eileen Heckart and Arthur Kennedy). These two are overwhelmed by Susan's almost identical resemblance to Veronica Brabissant, a long-dead daughter of the family for whom they work. Susan and Larry accompany the Mackeys to the Brabissant mansion to see a picture of Veronica, and there, in Veronica's room, which has been preserved as a shrine to her memory, Susan is induced to impersonate Veronica for a few minutes in order to solace the only surviving Brabissant, Veronica's addled sister who lives in the past and believes that Veronica is alive and angry with her. "Just say you're not angry with her," Mrs. Mackey instructs Susan. "It'll be such a blessin' for her!" But once Susan is dressed in Veronica's clothes, and Larry has been escorted downstairs by the Mackeys, Susan finds herself locked in the room and locked in the role of Veronica. Or is she really Veronica, in the year 1935, pretending to be an imaginary Susan?

> The play's twists and turns are, in the words of another critic, "like finding yourself trapped in someone else's nightmare," and "the climax is as jarring as it is surprising." "Neat and elegant thriller."—*Village Voice.*

ROYALTY, $50–$35

MY FAT FRIEND

CHARLES LAURENCE

(Little Theatre) Comedy

3 Men, 1 Woman, Interior

Vicky, who runs a bookshop in Hampstead, is a heavyweight. Inevitably she suffers, good-humouredly enough, the slings and arrows of the two characters who share the flat over the shop; a somewhat glum Scottish youth who works in an au pair capacity, and her lodger, a not-so-young homosexual. When a customer—a handsome bronzed man of thirty—seems attracted to her she resolves she will slim by hook or by crook. Aided by her two friends, hard exercise, diet and a graph, she manages to reduce to a stream-lined version of her former self—only to find that it was her rotundity that attracted the handsome book-buyer in the first place. When, on his return, he finds himself confronted by a sylph his disappointment is only too apparent. The newly slim Vicky is left alone once more, to be consoled (up to a point) by her effeminate lodger.

> "My fat Friend is abundant with laughs."—*Times Newsmagazine.* "If you want to laugh go."—*WCBS-TV.*

ROYALTY, $50–$35

PROMENADE, ALL!

DAVID V. ROBISON

(Little Theatre) Comedy

3 Men, 1 Woman, Interior

Four actors play four successive generations of the same family, as their business grows from manufacturing buttons to a conglomerate of international proportions (in the U.S. their perfume will be called Belle Nuit; but in Paris, Enchanted Evening). The Broadway cast included Richard Backus, Anne Jackson, Eli Wallach and Hume Cronyn. Miss Jackson performed as either mother or grandmother, as called for; and Cronyn and Wallach alternated as fathers and grandfathers; with Backus playing all the roles of youth. There are some excellent cameos to perform, such as the puritanical mother reading the Bible to her son without realizing the sexual innuendoes; or the 90-year-old patriarch who is agreeable to trying an experiment in sexology but is afraid of a heart attack.

> "So likeable; jolly and splendidly performed."—*N.Y. Daily News.* "The author has the ability to write amusing lines, and there are many of them."—*N.Y. Post.* "Gives strong, lively actors a chance for some healthy exercise. And what a time they have at it!"—*CBS-TV.*

ROYALTY, $50–$35

ACCOMMODATIONS

NICK HALL

(Little Theatre) Comedy

2 Men, 2 Women, Interior

Lee Schallert, housewife, feeling she may be missing out on something, leaves her husband, Bob, and her suburban home and moves into a two-room Greenwich Village apartment with two roommates. One roommate, Pat, is an aspiring actress, never out of characters or costumes, but, through an agency mix up, the other roommate is a serious, young, graduate student—male. The ensuing complications make a hysterical evening.

> "An amusing study of marital and human relations . . . a gem . . . It ranks as one of the funniest ever staged."—*Labor Herald.* "The audience at Limestone Valley Dinner Theater laughed at "Accommodations" until it hurt."—*News American.* "Superior theater, frivolous, perhaps, but nonetheless superior. It is light comedy at its best."—*The Sun, Baltimore.*

ROYALTY, $50–25

THE GOOD DOCTOR

NEIL SIMON

(All Groups) Comedy

2 Men, 3 Women. Various settings.

With Christopher Plummer in the role of the Writer, we are introduced to a composite of Neil Simon and Anton Chekhov, from whose short stories Simon adapted the capital vignettes of this collection. Frances Sternhagen played, among other parts, that of a harridan who storms a bank and upbraids the manager for his gout and lack of money. A father takes his son to a house where he will be initiated into the mysteries of sex, only to relent at the last moment, and leave the boy more perplexed than ever. In another sketch a crafty seducer goes to work on a wedded woman, only to realize that the woman has been in command from the first overture. Let us not forget the classic tale of a man who offers to drown himself for three rubles. The stories are droll, the portraits affectionate, the humor infectious, and the fun unending.

"As smoothly polished a piece of work as we're likely to see all season."—*N.Y. Daily News.* "A great deal of warmth and humor —vaudevillian humor—in his retelling of these Chekhovian tales."—*Newhouse Newspapers.* "There is much fun here . . . Mr. Simon's comic fancy is admirable."—*N.Y. Times.*

$1.75 (Music available. Write for particulars.)
ROYALTY, $50–$35

The Prisoner of Second Avenue

NEIL SIMON

(All Groups) Comedy

2 Men, 4 Women, Interior

Mel is a well-paid executive of a fancy New York company which has suddenly hit the skids and started to pare the payroll. Anxiety doesn't help; Mel, too, gets the ax. His wife takes a job to tide them over, then she too is sacked. As if this weren't enough, Mel is fighting a losing battle with the very environs of life. Polluted air is killing everything that grows on his terrace; the walls of the high-rise apartment are paper-thin, so that the private lives of a pair of German stewardesses next door are open books to him; the apartment is burgled; and his psychiatrist dies with $23,000 of his money. Mel does the only thing left for him to do: he has a nervous breakdown. It is on recovery that we come to esteem him all the more. For Mel and his wife and people like them have the resilience, the grit to survive.

"Now all this, mind you, is presented primarily in humorous terms."—*N.Y. Daily News.* "A gift for taking a grave subject and, without losing sight of its basic seriousness, treating it with hearty but sympathetic humor . . . A talent for writing a wonderfully funny line . . . full of humor and intelligence . . . Fine fun."—*N.Y. Post.* "Creates an atmosphere of casual cataclysm, and everyday urban purgatory of copelessness from which laughter seems to be released like vapor from the city's manholes."—*Time.*

$1.75. ROYALTY, $50–$35

A COMMUNITY OF TWO

JEROME CHODOROV

(All Groups) Comedy

4 Men, 3 Women, Interior

Winner of a Tony Award for "Wonderful Town." Co-author of "My Sister Eileen," "Junior Miss," "Anniversary Waltz." This is a charming off-beat comedy about Alix Carpenter, a fortyish divorceè of one month who has been locked out of her own apartment and is rescued by her thrice-divorced neighbor across the hall, Michael Jardeen. During the course of the two hours in which it takes to play out the events of the evening, we meet Alix's ex-husband, a stuffed shirt from Wall Street, her son, who has run away from prep school with his girl, heading for New Mexico and a commune, Michael's current girl friend, Olga, a lady anthropologist just back from Lapland, and Mr. Greenberg, a philosopher-locksmith. All take part in the hilarious doings during a blizzard that rages outside the building and effects everybody's lives. But most of all, and especially, we get to know the eccentric Michael Jardeen, and the confused and charming Alix Carpenter, who discover that love might easily happen, even on a landing, in the course of a couple of hours of high-stress living.

"Thoroughly delightful comedy."—*St. Louis-Post Dispatch*. "A joy."—*Cleveland Plain Dealer*. "Skillful fun by Jerome Chodorov."—*Toronto Globe Star*.

ROYALTY, $50–$35

ROMAN CONQUEST

JOHN PATRICK

(All Groups) Comedy

One set—3 Women, 6 Men

The romantic love story of two American girls living in the romantic city of Rome in a romantic garret at the foot of the famous Spanish steps. One of the world's richest young women takes her less fortunate girl friend to Italy to hide unknown and escape notoriety while she attempts to discover if she has any talent as an artist—free of position and prestige. Their misadventures with language and people supply a delightful evening of pure entertainment. Remember the movies "Three Coins in the Fountain" and "Love Is A Many Splendored Thing"? This new comedy is in the same vein by the same Pulitzer Prize winning playwright.

ROYALTY, $50–$35

Other Comedies by
Jack Sharkey

(all single-set, 3-act, modern dress)

HERE LIES JEREMY TROY
(3 men, 2 women)

*M IS FOR THE MILLION
(from 7 men, 4 women to 13 men, 5 women)

KISS OR MAKE UP
(4 men, 3 women)

HOW GREEN WAS MY BROWNIE
(6 men, 5 women)

MEANWHILE, BACK ON THE COUCH . . .
(4 men, 4 women)

A GENTLEMAN AND A SCOUNDREL
(2 men, 1 woman)

SPINOFF
(3 men, 3 women)

* (listed as 2-act play, but adaptable to 3 acts)

SAMUEL FRENCH, Inc.

25 West 45th St.   7623 Sunset Blvd.
NEW YORK 10036   HOLLYWOOD 90046

#11

HOME-BUILT

Lighting Equipment

for The Small Stage
By THEODORE FUCHS

This volume presents a series of fourteen simplified designs
for building various types of stage lighting and control equip-
ment, with but one purpose in mind—to enable the amateur
producer to acquire a complete set of stage lighting equip-
ment at the lowest possible cost. The volume is 8½″ x 11″ in
size, with heavy paper and spiral binding—features which
make the volume well suited to practical workshop use.

$3.50

Community Theatre

A MANUAL FOR SUCCESS

By JOHN WRAY YOUNG

The ideal text for anyone interested in participating in Community Theatre as a vocation or avocation. "Organizing a
Community Theatre," "A Flight Plan for the Early Years,"
"Programming for People—Not Computers," and other chap-
ters are blueprints for solid growth. "Technical, Business and
Legal Procedures" cuts a safe and solvent path through some
tricky undergrowth. Essential to the library of all community
theatres, and to the schools who will supply them with talent
in the years to come.

$3.00